FAMILY

ALSO BY JOY LADIN

POETRY

Impersonation [2022]

Shekhinah Speaks [2022]

The Future Is Trying to Tell Us Something:
New and Selected Poems [2017]

Fireworks in the Graveyard [2017]

Impersonation [2015]

The Definition of Joy [2012]

Coming to Life [2010]

Psalms [2010]

Transmigration [2009]

The Book of Anna [2006]

Alternatives to History [2003]

MEMOIR

Through the Door Life: a Jewish Journey Between Genders [2011]

TRANS THEOLOGY

The Soul of the Stranger:
Reading God and Torah from a Transgender Perspective [2018]

FAMILY

POEMS

JOY LADIN

A Karen & Michael Braziller Book
PERSEA BOOKS / NEW YORK

PERSEA BOOKS, INC.
90 Broad Street
New York, New York 10004

Library of Congress Control Number: 2024940249

Book design and composition by Rita Skingle
Typeset in Minion
Manufactured in the United States of America.
Printed on acid-free paper.

In memory of my mother,
LOLA KIPNIS LADIN, LEAH BAT RIVKA,
who taught me to say "family"

MARCH 9, 1930–JUNE 13, 2022

CONTENTS

AUTOBIOGRAPHY OF MY WHITENESS

HAIKU SUITES

In memory of Lola Kipnis Ladin

Four Seasons

Three owls hoot and answer
the last full moon
of a year of love and terror.

*

Heavy spring rain. No matter who wraps them,
my mother's legs
keep weeping.

*

For the first time this summer,
I'm not wrong
when I hear water falling.

*

Wind in the branches, someone's mother
calling, someone else's childhood
skipping from yard to yard.

Autumn / Mother / Rain

We look at pictures on a rainy day. For the first time
my mother fails to recognize
in a photograph, my face.

*

Rain fine as flour
falling through a sieve. So this is what it feels like
to forgive.

*

I fall asleep to rain
sshhing
like a mother

*

I don't know who or how to ask
what that bird's saying
to the rain

*

How long did it take Noah
to worry about his mother
when it started to rain

*

Raining so hard
my mother knows
I'm not coming today

*

Dark the next morning,
my mother calls, train whistle
fading in the rain

Last Spring

As winter melts into spring
my mother keeps asking
when summer will end

*

I wasn't the healthiest child
she says
How did I get so old

*

Spring in the courtyard
My mother tells me how lonely she is
She still remembers that

*

I see her organs failing
in the sunset colors
of her swollen lower lids

*

Robin please before it's too late
remind my mother
it's spring

Summering

All night, two cicadas
call and answer
across the unmown yard

*

Sleep
rustles through your body, wind
through moonlit corn

*

I wake in your arms
to a chipmunk repeating
the only word it knows

*

All the branches shake at once
then silence
leaves and sun

*

Car horn, cardinal, potato frying—
It's not just me, today
the world sounds happy

Mid-Summer

Only at sunset I notice—
the lilac's leaves
reflect the sky

*

Bird chirping,
thickening cloud, next-door neighbor
mowing

*

One window full of leaves, the other
full of sky. Mid-July. Still time
to grow up before I die.

*

Black chestnut ripples
like fur
on a sleeping cat

*

Tonight for once
I was paying attention
when the insects started singing

*

Here I am
trying to give up
and you keep blossoming

End of Summer

Sitting on the stoop, the mist
kissing the crowns of trees
also kisses me

*

Surprises me every year
the way greens deepen
as leaves grow old

*

Monarch, what are you waiting for
on that plume
of pampas?

*

Like sunset, some pain
glows for hours
after the sun is gone

*

Need to pee
but I hate to walk out
while that cicada's talking

III. IN THE NEW PLACE

Disability

I stare at the trees that line my street
the way old sailors
stare at the sea

*

Time to get used to wearing
mortality
on my sleeve

*

The needle, as always, goes in
Today, clouds
fill the syringe

*

Sun on my face, twittering birds
and time
to notice them

*

What a relief to see
how little the world
depends on me

*

The first leaves sidle down, feathers
from a bird of gold
who flies by letting go

Before Moving

How strange to feel
a place I am
become a place I've been

*

What do they know
that I don't—
the clouds that aren't moving?

*

In these boxes—
birth certificate, will,
and everything in between

*

Thought it was the night
but it was my own skin
sweating

*

Lawn mower roar recedes
and then it's just me
and the insects, singing

In the New Place

Heaped on shelves, clothes I no longer need
remember the body
that wore them

*

On this street
nothing reminds me
of my children

*

Shadows
like someone else's family
gather in the hall

*

I believe with perfect faith
the birds that sound so far away
are really right outside

*

Echo of my childhood—
windchimes
on a shadowless afternoon

*

If I stare at you
all night
will you look like home

Windows

I raise my shade
Across the street
a neighbor's doorbell rings

*

Ready for winter
pine branches piled
with snow-colored sky

*

Burst of birdsong
beyond the pane
Sound of a small plane landing

*

Sun strikes the window across the stairs
ricochets
through the dust of mine

*

Growing old growing young
my skin says yes
to November sun

*

How long have I been here
up to my neck in sunshine
splashing across my bed

*

When I open the window
light and voices
enter with the cold

FAMILY

Sick Psalm

You're more than my illness
the sick thing says

to the God whose illness
the universe is

I love you more
than I hate

my dizziness
my forgetfulness

I feel you walking toward me
across burning skin

The closer you come
the sicker I get

Come in the sick thing says
There's a room inside my illness

a bed and a table
a glass of water

a room where dying
sounds like laughter

where your always
kisses

my before and after

Letter to the Lord

Lord quite innocent of what it is to live
bound in paper, bound in steel,
bound in the incredible ignorance supplied
by irony and suffering,

I regret that I am unable to see you,
wrapped as I am
in time, soiled and sickened
by personal situations,

struggling to find you
among your misprints
and translations, broken tablets, shredded scrolls,
weathering epitaphs,

Otherwise, I'm fine,
unable to see you
but ready to shut my eyes
and feel my way

through the cemetery of your longing—
or is it mine?—
for someone else
to be responsible for life.

You live too much
and I live too, one of innumerable
lines you true,
rubbed and mounted by the dark

I tell myself is you.

A Friendly Visit with God

How was *your* day?
No, don't tell me:

there was evening, there was morning,
you had a hell of a time

disentangling light from darkness,
consciousness from slime.

You want to talk,
but your voice, frankly,

makes me feel like a bush on fire.
It would be better

if I could look you in the face
without dying.

I'm sure it's a nice face.
I'm sure you wish

once in a while
someone would tell you that.

It's sad that you can't go out to dinner,
snap a selfie, forget.

You're here, I'm here,
and you can't understand

why I can't understand
what you're really saying

and I can't remember why
I thought tonight would go better.

When I think you're gone,
part of me starts crying

please turn on the light.

Whisper

I didn't know
I was in prison

till I looked out
the small round windows

and saw you whispering stars

Hannah, Whose Son Was Lent to the Lord

> For as long as he lives he is lent to the LORD.
>   I Samuel 1:28

You learned to tell stories
that would never end
as long as you kept saying "and."

I tried to pay attention
but knew I would forget
even though, or maybe because,

I tried to memorize
every word you said.
I knew the Lord

would take you back.
That when I put you to my breast,
I was feeding a debt.

That is the way of the Lord.
The barren woman's womb is opened.
The mother is bereft.

I grew as you grew.
Laughed when you laughed.
Took you up to the house of the Lord.

Led you by the hand. In dreams
from which I wake
bathed in sweat

I am sometimes permitted to see you,
sometimes even to kiss
your head that smells like sun-warmed clover

while you look straight ahead.

There

You help around the house
we've never shared,

sometimes singing, sometimes quiet,
sometimes ablaze with anger.

Apples burn in your orchard.
Teapot shrieks above your ring of fire.

You can't see me, but I'm there,
in the midst of the conflagration

that's all that remains
of our life together.

I know you don't think about that
though I don't know much about you now,

what you eat, who you love,
whether you answered

college application questions
about hardships overcome

by describing the incendiary
umbilical cord

whose burning still ties you
to me, the parent you can't see,

in whom you never grew,
whose love for you still blazes

like flame among blossoms.

The Last Time I Saw Him

he pretended I wasn't there
We were inches apart

when he opened the door
It was morning or maybe afternoon

Cool but sunny spring or early fall
His eyes never flickered toward my face

Hovered in the space
over my right shoulder

He must have seen
the stubbly fields behind me

and maybe the tree
and maybe the treehouse

where ghosts of childhoods
unscarred by me

eternally snack
on ghosts of apple and cheese

I kept smiling up at him
as though he'd answered my greeting

hoping I'm ashamed to say
to see some strain in his face

some struggle not to notice
the parent he erased

In the house behind him
a dog was barking

In the paddock
beside the muddy pond

two slow horses
paid no attention

when he turned his back

Thirteen Ways of Looking at a Summer

1

Final test results are in, and the specialist, seeing neither progress
nor treatment options, is no longer interested. That means these
are the good old days, days when I can still get out of bed, wash
myself, walk downstairs, drive now and then. When I have energy
to do and lament the work of being disabled: applications to fill
out and blanks to fill in, plans to make and plans to cancel, losses
to anticipate, wheelchairs to price, facts to face, clichès to mock,
clichès to embrace, squirrels to envy as they leap from tree to tree.

2

At midnight, the moment the 17th becomes the 18th of July, my
tenured teaching position ends. Not much changes. Insects keep
whirring, humidity sweating, stars non-committally burning, as
the possessives I clung to as I got sicker—*my* title, *my* office, *my*
students, *my* classes—dissolve into damp night air.

3

The landlord says I have to move. I'm lying in bed—I almost
always am—when I get the news. The bedroom, like my job,
immediately starts slipping into the past, but the bed is still here,
carrying me like a raft toward bedroom-less waters where I can no
longer see a future.

4

Somewhere or other, every week, once-in-a-generation storms,
hundred-year floods, incineration of nation-sized stands of
wilderness, but last week's hurricane barely brushed us. No rabbis
drowned in their cars; no families drowned in basements.

5

A half hour here, five minutes there, my past disappears. It's never long before I'm exhausted. But piles grow smaller. Class notes, syllabi, attendance rosters bagged as trash along with thrift-store remnants of gender transition—junk jewelry, unopened makeup, clothing for women I didn't turn out to be. Books boxed along with drafts of old poems and a few surviving scraps of childhoods outgrown by children I won't see again.

6

My mother keeps falling every few weeks, so she's moved to assisted living, where, on her very first morning, she falls again. One foot moves; the other doesn't. An instant later, her nose is shattered, her knees and forehead split. Another stretcher. Another ambulance. Her caregivers say the moment before she fell, she was happy. I sit beside her emergency room bed, waiting to learn what's broken inside her. She can't remember where she was, or is. Did something happen, she asks.

7

I tell and retell the story of her life. Each time, she listens with interest, and, a few dozen heartbeats later, asks me to tell her again.

8

Not long after her release, my mother tests positive and is locked in her apartment. I keep her company through a video screen. Now and then, in the background, someone in a white hazmat suit washes dishes my mother doesn't remember are there.

9

Then it's the end of August. Liz carries boxes of surplus past
downstairs to tag sale tables. I lie in bed, the unmoved mover,
invisible center of attention.

10

That evening, a fleeting resurrection: I get dressed for the first
time in days and we go out to dinner. Fries and onion rings by the
bucket at a place on route 47, part greenhouse, part sugar shack,
part watering hole for local farmers.

We sit outside, under an awning. A few yards away, potted rows
of purple, blue, and crimson flowers. One table over, four white
women (a category I worked hard, with mixed results, to join) and
one equally white but deeply sunburned man. They've known one
another for years, drink and laugh about a misadventure buying
chickens. "Turned out to be layers, so I won't be killing them
for the party," the storyteller laughs. We laugh too, inhaling and
exhaling flowers that won't stop growing, the smell of fried food,
strangers' voices, the thickening glow of evening. The glow before
the gloaming.

No gunshots in earshot. No one visibly suffering for or adjacent
to our pleasure. A stand of willows screens the swollen river, the
late sun dangling above them, as though we'd all been here forever,
watching summer end.

11

Liz smiles across the table. She's leaving tomorrow. I'll pack more
boxes and stare out my bedroom windows—the new place doesn't
get much light—remembering the first summer we were together,
the miles I walked every evening for pleasure, the mountains
flushed, then bruised, then fireflies flashing in the short-lived
celebrity of darkness and bats like black flags fluttering above
my head.

Less carbon in the atmosphere then. Fewer extinctions per
minute. Fewer blanks in my mother's head.

12

A few weeks later, my apartment no longer is. I move one town
west, from Nipmuc to Nonotuck land. Two bedrooms, wood
floors, galley kitchen, full bath. A porch with a couple of plastic
chairs. A halfway house across the street, flanked by shaggy pines.

Strips of fading lawn and flower bed, low brick buildings,
enormous wooden houses with narrow asphalt drives. The street
is only one block long. Downtown at one end, cemetery at the
other.

13

I sit on the porch a few minutes a day. Get some sun on my face.
Summer's not quite over. I still believe that someday soon, I'll walk
down the steps and around the corner.

And just like that,

my mother is dying. My mother has been dying for years, my mother, like me, was always dying, but today my mother's failing clock of a heart lurched ahead toward stopping. Too much beating, too little breathing. Too much sweating, too much urinating, too little oxygen, too little sleeping. The hospice nurse says my mother has been given morphine and is resting. The woman who helped her through the night weeps into the mask it isn't safe to stop wearing.

My mother's saying goodbye one organ at a time. Her eyes and mine keep leaking. Yesterday she was sitting up and talking, forgetting every word we were saying, yes, but she was breathing. When I arrived it was raining. The screens on her windows dim with drops caught as they were falling.

Overnight, spring's become summer—heat, blossoming, birds which since 4 am have not for a moment stopped singing. There has never since the beginning of the world been a more beautiful morning. A morning more inseparable from mourning.

By the time I reach my mother, she's once more breathing normally, but, for the first time, wearing pajamas in the afternoon.

I say, as though I care, that spring has suddenly become summer. "Is it almost Christmas?" my mother asks. Time means something different to her now. It always has. Some other kind of love bound us across a continent we rarely crossed, decades we didn't share. Love that when I were young—suddenly, I feel young again—
I called loneliness.

My Mother's Body

is busy shutting down.
Eyelids flutter. Heartbeat slows. I can almost feel
her dark red chambers
emptying and filling.

My mother smiles in her sleep. Maybe a spasm. Maybe a dream.
Maybe she knows I'm there.
Hears my voice. Is dreaming
we're together. Her mouth

a gaping Gothic arch,
gateway to a house
struggling to stay haunted.
Some of her's still in there.

My sister says the funeral
can be whatever I want.
I find it hard to want
a funeral for my mother,

a box and a body
and a hole in the ground.
It's my job to imagine
the funeral that is striding closer, the hole

that has already opened
in the days ahead.
To decide what to say
above the body.

To think "the body"
about my mother.
It's my job to remember
all the jobs that I'm not doing.

My mother is far away and shrinking
like a sliver of sky
through closing shades.
Her chin sinks to her chest.

I repeat words my mother won't remember
and can only occasionally understand.
My sister says
her status is changing fast.

Suddenly, clearly,
my mother asks what's happening.
My sister explains as she has so often
that she, our mother, is dying.

It's my job to explain that too. Another job
I'm not doing.
My mother's eyelids flutter open.
The light in her eyes comes on,

she smiles her famous smile
of delight, of inside jokes, of triumph,
and turns her head from my sister to me.
Well *that* was an experience, she says.

Mourning

I wake, almost,
from a dream
in which I am down on all fours, forehead pressed
to a patch of ice. In the dream

my mother is strapped to my back. As I wake
I still feel her behind me,
weighing almost nothing.
The part of me that's still asleep

tells her I love her. The part of her
strapped to my back
does not reply. In the dream I know
that though she's there, attached to me and dying,

she's also sobbing
in the afterlife. I walk through
a roomful of people
murmuring her name

into an unknown city's summer. That's
when I start crying,
sink to all fours, press my forehead
to an inexplicable patch

of summer ice. Someone's asking
if I prefer butter or noodles.
I don't understand the question.
My attention is on my mother

sobbing in the afterlife
about the hands
she no longer has.
I thought you were going to take care of her,

I say to God. God,
like my mother,
doesn't answer.
I try to stop falling

awake, to keep feeling
the weight
of her vanishing.

Flesh

Every day since you died, I feel
my flesh. I try not to.
I used to be good at that—

not feeling.
Not saying to myself, This
is my flesh,

these holes, this hairy distended dome
atop a rickety tower of bone
rising from a bed.

Not feeling was my superpower. Feeling
is the opposite.
You often told me how lonely you felt

but not about your flesh,
the pain—
I know there was pain—

the bruises that never went away,
skin splitting open on your legs, the breath
you increasingly couldn't catch.

For decades you told me,
as though you never had,
that you were numb on one side.

It wasn't a superpower - a virus did that.
Even when your body no longer bothered
to store calories as fat

and your clothes were all too big,
you were careful not to eat desserts.
You'd lost a lot of weight

and swore you'd never gain it back.
By the end, your only mirror
was above the bathroom sink. Others

kept your eyebrows drawn,
washed you in the shower,
dried and dressed your flesh.

I never asked and you never said
if their care
felt like love

or the way yours felt
when, before school, you brushed my hair flat
or forced into shirts and pants,

pushing and pulling
until I looked like the child
you wished you had.

In your dying months
you'd kiss my cheek
when I would come,

sometimes hold my hand.
It always took me
by surprise,

you wanting to feel my flesh.
Saying you loved me.
Me saying it back.

I knew it meant you were dying.
I kept my eyes on your face
and tried not to feel

the way I had as a child.
Easier for you, easier for me,
if I didn't feel

held down, paralyzed, suffocated
by flesh.
But since your death, I can't not feel

the body you left me in,
the old
overwhelming sadness

of torso, groin, and skin.
When I was growing up,
you told me you'd had a miscarriage

a year or two before I was born.
I used to wonder why the boy you lost
hadn't been born instead.

I felt your love
as you were dying
one memory at a time

when you squeezed my hand.
It *was* love,
I'm sure of it,

and not just fear or loneliness,
but I still don't understand
what kind of love we shared.

I don't know if that matters.
I knew you were dying
and you knew I was there,

and so was love,
yours and mine,
tangled like fingers together.

1. Abney Garden Park Cemetery

I rest on a bench
between leaning crypts

undermined and overgrown
by hawthorne roots and ivy,

making myself at home
among eroding angels

and moss-blurred epitaphs.
You're in your element,

snapping photographs,
deciphering grandiloquent expressions

of love, virtue, faith in resurrection.
Goldcrest and chiffchaff

wing from branch to branch.
Brevity and brilliance,

grief and acceptance,
in a single sun-struck glance.

We're surrounded by fungi—slime molds, jelly ears,
yellowbrains, blushing rosettes—

fattening on Victorian arsenic and lead
in the hollowed-out trunks

of this urban forest
that meant to be a garden.

The pandemic won't start for a couple of years
so it's easy to feel

life has triumphed over death,
overgrown and walled it in,

arranged it into artful paths,
resting places, granite slabs,

snippets of wilderness.
This is the perfect place

to feel how tired I am,
amid nineteenth-century dissidents

and species that have trembled for decades
on the lip of extinction

like hairs in a thinning mustache.
Rustle and thud

in the underbrush.
I smile back at you across the graves.

Not me. Not here. Not yet.

2. Winter Anniversary

Wings of an angel
with two hearts

and two heads,
we lean out the window

into a night
cold, familial and fragile

as the cheek of a mother
made of glass.

It's the night after the night
you came back.

Moonlight bright
as fresh-fallen snow

glories the frozen grass.

3. Sheltering in Place

waiting for corn to sprout, lilacs to open,
white supremacy to be dismantled

and the apolitical
whiteness of clouds

to inch across the sky;
for sleep to spread

from your leg to mine;
for the dog to tell us

pizza's arrived;
for notebooks to fill

and characters to become lives
and words that aren't mine

to arrange themselves
into the voice of the divine;

for cities to reopen,
treatments to work,

blood to fill
the right-hand chamber of my heart

even when I'm upright;
for chipmunks and buzzards,

black squirrels, snapping turtles,
great blue herons, mockingbirds and foxes;

for something that feels like summer
to remind us

of shades of green we have forgotten
and phosphorescent insects to rise

from the grounds of the house
that isn't ours

to the story we inhabit,
the story of Sabbaths

lingering in the sky,
spooning bodies, carmelized onions,

gusts of rain through window screens;
symptoms that don't subside;

walks I can no longer take;
flashes of firefly.

4. When You're in New York

You walk through the world and I walk too,
shrinking and stretching inside your shadow,
glinting like sun on your glasses.

A bus is kneeling at a shelter
and look, I'm the shelter
and also the driver

kneeling thoughtfully in case you want to enter
then roaring off
through the city that loves you

almost as much as I do,
posing for your pictures, trying to look familiar,
trying to look brand new,

leading you through turns and tunnels
to the treasures cloistered
in the oldest layers,

rocks and shells and bits of paper,
bones and wounds
for you to discover.

Whatever I have been or done
is yours.
You're the center of my map,

the sun I bask in beside the turtles,
the neighborhood I grew up in,
the little place

no one else will ever find
where you and I
are drinking wine

and falling in love again.

Trying to Write About the Torah

Please don't elect a dictator

when I'm trying to write about the Torah.
The Torah's ways are paths of peace,
underground streams
that never run dry

or overflow

no matter how the climate changes
so it's hard to write about the Torah
as forests burn
and seas swallow island nations

when the Torah is an unsinkable ark

preserving at least two versions
of every kind of truth
to populate whatever worlds emerge
when waters recede or part

and it's hard to write about a Torah that floats

on waves of extinction,
genuses and species, plants and peoples, lives
we're happy to live, futures
we can bear to imagine,

when, a few verses after the Flood,

the very first rainbow
is already shining,
Pharoah sinking, millions of slaves
celebrating the first Juneteenth.

It's hard to write about the Torah

when the Torah and the world
are written on one another,
black fire and white fire.
When both are always burning.

When the world keeps turning

to ashes and smoke
and the Torah
is not consumed.

Sitting in Wordsworth's Garden

where you sat
iambicizing childhood, revolution, and the Terror,
I inhale the scent

of virtues you knew
would bloom
even when forgotten by the future

sitting in your garden
in a sweat-stained sleeveless dress
trying to come up with something to say—

flowers? clouds? loneliness?—
unable to make poetry,
unable to make sense

and unable to say nothing
as my country cages children
who may not survive the growing season.

No matter how many are caged or killed,
your garden's short-lived citizens,
rosa mundi, apothecary rose, common valerian,

annually perform
their parable of resistance.
Die and blossom again.

No one expects them to rhyme
beauty with justice, stamens
with the fear

that's coated my country like pollen
since the last election. People
are thrown in cages

and poets like me, alive and afraid, conscious
and unconscious, singular
and symptomatic,

scan heaven and earth
and flower bed
for an arc that bends toward justice

and something eloquent,
original, and vague—
something a flower might say—

that makes liberty sound inevitable and safe
and tyranny destined to pass away.
Poems aren't keys

that unlock cages,
just strings of letters
on screens or pages

hoping some future
will read them and remember
that somewhere there was a garden

and somewhere there still is,
inexcusably rhyming
beauty with existence

in a language that has no words
for justice or injustice,
complicity or cages.

In pastel plosives; violet vowels;
half-blown roses'
luminous consonance.

A Bridge on Account of Sex:
A Trans Woman Speaks to Susan B. Anthony on
the 100th Anniversary of the 19th Amendment

We hold these truths to be self-evident . . .
      (Declaration of Independence, 1776)

The right of citizens of the United States to vote shall not be
denied or abridged by the United States or by any State on
account of sex.
      (Amendment XIX, 1920)

      I

In Rochester, New York,
you were buried and I was born,
and both of us voted
for the very first time, and we—
may I include you in my "we"?—
were both denied and abridged

on account of sex
by the same United States
that wrapped us in the privilege
perversely accorded
the whiteness of our skins
and told us we were nothing

but what our bodies said.
You weren't having that.
You were determined to not only vote
but to get sent to jail
and that wasn't easy for a white lady like you,
well-schooled and well-connected.

First, you had to bully
the barbershop election inspectors
into voter registration.
Hair was being cut,
razors stropped,
the beards of patriarchy trimmed,

and the boys weren't moved by your citation
of the 14th Amendment and the New York Constitution
until you threatened legal action.

You had a judge behind you, you said.
You did. Thirteen registered women later,
a panicked newspaper proclaimed,

"Citizenship no more carries the right to vote
than the right to fly to the moon."
"Well I have been and gone and done it!!"
you wrote your bff, Elizabeth Cady ("Mrs.") Stanton—
not flown to the moon, but "positively voted"
on November 5th, 1872. A week and a half later,

a warrant was issued for your arrest
for voting while female
(maximum penalty: three years imprisonment).
A deputy marshal appeared in your parlor
wearing a beaver hat; said the weather was fine

(not likely, given the beaver hat
and Rochester in November)
and invited you (a white lady, after all)
to call on the election commissioner.
"Is that the way you arrest men?" you asked. Demanded
to be led out in handcuffs.

You won that argument too.
The embarrassed young man
brought you, you would later say,
to "the same dingy little room
where fugitive slaves
were examined and returned to their masters."

A grand jury was impaneled.
You were delighted,
and twice refused bail,
hoping to be imprisoned.
Not in a skin like yours.
Your own attorney bailed you out,

because, he said, "I could not see a lady I respected"
(you were white, after all)
put in jail." On the plus side,
the grand jury, twenty men,
indicted you for voting, the charges read,
being then and there, as you well knew,

a person of the female sex,
possessor of a body
that could only be enfranchised
contrary to the statute, and against the peace
of the United States of America.
In a grey silk dress, white lace collar, neatly knotted hair,

you spent the months before your trial
giving speeches the prosecutor feared
would persuade every potential juror
to find you innocent.
He needn't have worried.
The Supreme Court had narrowed the 14th Amendment

to preserve the right to discriminate
on the basis of sex.
The judge sustained the objection
that you, as a woman,
were "not competent" to testify
about your own opinions;

barred you from taking the stand;
cut the trial short
by reading the guilty verdict he'd written
before it began.
He didn't let the jurors say a word
but though he kept trying,

he couldn't keep you from declaring
that you'd been convicted according to laws
written, interpreted and applied
by and for the very same men
who, not long before, had made it a crime,
"punishable with a $1,000 fine

and six months imprisonment"
to give a fugitive slave
a swallow of water or crust of bread.
"As the slaves who got their freedom," you said,
"over, or under, or through
the unjust forms of law,

now, must women, to get their right
to a voice in this government,
take it."

Over every objection, you did.

II

In Rochester, New York,
a century later,
in the America you insisted
had no right
not to exist—slavery abolished, voting rights
unabridgeable, at least on paper,

on account of race or sex—
I was born
to a card-carrying member
of your twentieth-century daughters,
the League of Women Voters. My mother
who thought I was her son

taught me nothing about being a woman
but she taught me to vote
and drive a stick;
stand up for myself in supermarkets;
speak in a low voice
(she'd trained for radio)

and showed me how to live
without being ashamed
of being curly, freckled, Jewish, mouthy,
different.
A magazine on her nightstand
taught me the word for what I am

though it was forty years
before she heard me say it,
a word *you* never learned
because it didn't exist
for a way of being human
you couldn't imagine.

I guess I'm not a truth
you'd hold self-evident.
I wonder if you'd say
I, like you, was created equal,
was created at all, in fact,
or would write me off as yet another outrage

perpetrated by men,
or would see me refusing, like you,
to be what others said,
and tell me, as my mother did,
"Whatever you look like,
you'll always be my child."

No. You wouldn't say that.
You didn't have people like me in mind
when you fought your country to redefine
what it means to be a woman,
but here we are
and here I am,

abridged, like you, on account of sex,
wrapped, like you,
in education, money, and whiteness
that have so far kept me from being jailed,
evicted, beaten, burned
or tossed in a ditch

as my sisters have
for defying, like you,
contrary to the statute and against the peace
of the United States of America
every decree and argument
that we are created less,

created to hide, created to cringe, created to accept
that we're excluded, by definition,
from the unabridgeable *We*
by whom, for whom,
you insisted,
America was created. We,

like you, refuse to be determined
by the bodies we were born in,
to accept assumptions and abide by laws
that deem us other and less
than who we know we are.

America needed you to refuse.
Asking as your daughter's daughter:
Does America need me too?

AUTOBIOGRAPHY
OF MY WHITENESS

Whiteness: A User's Manual

[T]he white race is *invented*—and in another, parallel universe, it would not have existed at all. But it *is* deep in the sense of shaping one's being, one's cognition, one's experience in the world ... Biologically fictitious, race becomes socially real ...
    Charles W. Mills

In this country American means **white**. Everybody else has to hyphenate.
    Toni Morrison

[White people] are, in effect, still trapped in a history which they do not understand; and until they understand it, they cannot be released from it.
    James Baldwin

If I take your race away, ... all you got is your little self, and what is that? What are you without racism? Are you any good? Are you still strong? Are you still smart? Do you still like yourself?
    Toni Morrison

I seemed to have lost all sense of proportion. Where did my body end and the crystal and white world begin? Thoughts evaded me, hiding in the vast stretch of clinical whiteness to which I seemed connected only by a scale of receding grays. ... I listened intensely, aware of the form and movement of sentences and grasping the now subtle rhythmical differences between progressions of sound that questioned and those that made a statement. But still their meanings were lost in the vast whiteness in which I myself was lost. ...

But we are all human, I thought, wondering what I meant.

The end is in the beginning and lies far ahead.
Ralph Ellison, *The Invisible Man*

White Christmas

"as if...whiteness, the whitening substance, and the material
which is whitened are one and the same thing."
            (Moses Maimonides, *Guide for the Perplexed*)

Today as every day Little Whiteness
opens the same present: a world

fashioned by hands
Little Whiteness never sees.

Little Whiteness believes
elves stay up all night

cobbling together the white white world
Little Whiteness unwraps.

No wonder Little Whiteness
wakes up happy every day.

As far as Little Whitness can see
whiteness and whitening

and the world which is whitened
are one and the same thing.

The Whiteness of Love

I remember the whiteness of my mother's love,
the coupon-clipping whiteness

of her lower-middle-class love,
the brown round injustice

of the pennies she clutched
in the white-knuckled fingers

of love. The white house
on the all-white street

of the all-white neighborhood
of our love. The whiteness

of her childhood Depression
and the whiteness of mine

shone like lights in a closet
we dared not open.

No one could look
at the motions we went through

and say they saw anything
but whiteness and love.

Even when we were alone,
whiteness kept us under surveillance.

Eyes disguised as carpet stains
watched my mother and I rehearse

the whiteness that was to me
invisible as love.

I played a child playing a child,
my mother a mother

stirring milk, vanilla, sugar and flour
into cupcake batter,

mixing the ingredients
of our white, white world

into the whiteness of love.

Autobiography of My Whiteness

1

My whiteness
not alabaster's or a picket fence's

Donald Trump's or my mother's
naturalized freckled

Canadian whiteness: *my*
Jewish but dermatologically correct

purse-clutching pearl-clutching
syllabus- and faculty-bleaching

deer-in-the-headlights
flake-in-a-snowstorm

melting-ice-floe whiteness

2

and I grew up together
conjoined

by a platonic pallor
no freckle blemish flush or tan

could rupture
whatever redness or brownness

dawn or dusk
variegated my epidermis

no one could tell
my whiteness and me apart

3

though my whiteness
was so much older

midwived my birth
fattened me on milk and curd

and when I was very young
whispered stories in the dark

about a world that belonged to me
a world in which I

was the only color
in which the skin I hated

(that's another story)
shone like a crown

making me better
keeping me from harm

until I fell asleep
in whiteness' arms

4

Whiteness shone

in every face I dreamed
the vampires bending over my bed

the zombies gnawing
the whiteness of my skin

In every nightmare
there were a lot of nightmares

whiteness was what I'd run to
whiteness what I'd flee

murderer and victim
detective and mystery

whiteness teaching me
dream by dream

to see while keeping my eyes closed
to walk while staying asleep

5

Whiteness was a museum
and my life a diorama

curated to exemplify
the kind of whiteness I represented

the kind of whiteness I lived
a few streets over from neighborhoods

where children and parents
were occasionally shot

My whiteness was the fires
that never started on my block

the guns not fired in my direction
the bodies burning beside me

on *de facto* segregated beaches
maintained by people

whose faces were shades
my whiteness assured me

I didn't need to see

6

Whiteness surrounded me

with neighborhoods doctors presidents
land a country a history

laws that were supposed to protect me
ideals of beauty

I could never achieve
because they weren't designed

for people like me
someone snuck you might say

under whiteness' wire
by grandparents who fled

Slavic nations whose pallor they shared
that treated them

as God-murdering misers
for what they called the Golden Land

ie a country that cared less
(though it still cared)

about their Jewishness
than their relative lack of pigment

a comparatively benign neglect
institutionalized a few decades later

when the ovens of mass extermination
cast such an unflattering light

on anti-Semitism
even at its most polite

so that their children and their children's children
ie me

were relocated
provisionally

from sweatshops and slums
to whiteness' suburbs

wrapped in loans and mortgages
voting rights police protection loosened covenants

in which it was officially
and unofficially made clear

that people with faces like mine
were to be treated

as human

7

And so my whiteness was born
long before I was

Decades before we met
and made a life together

whiteness gave itself to me
and now I return the favor

shrinking and stretching
as whiteness demands

bending over backwards
to meet whiteness' gaze

perfectly capable of feeling ashamed
wishing to apologize now and then

but ready and willing
to grow old

without trying to remember
imagine or create

a me my whiteness isn't
who whiteness doesn't sing to sleep

in whom whiteness doesn't thrive
a me

whose autobiography cannot begin
until I stop repeating

the story of my whiteness
until my whiteness ends